THIS PAWSOME BOOK BELONGS TO:

PAW Patrol™: Annual 2020

A CENTUM BOOK 978-1-913072-29-2

Published in Great Britain by Centum Books Ltd

This edition published 2019

1 3 5 7 9 10 8 6 4 2

Centum Books Ltd, 20 Devon Square, Newton Abbot, Devon, TQ12 2HR, UK

books@centumbooksltd.co.uk

CENTUM BOOKS Limited Reg. No. 07641486

A CIP catalogue record for this book is available from the British Library

Printed in China.

ANNUAL
2020

centum

CONTENTS

WELCOME TO ADVENTURE BAY!

High paw, pup fans! Get ready for puzzle missions and activity challenges in every corner of Adventure Bay. Chase, Marshall, Skye and all the pups are here to help, so put your best paw forward and LET'S GET STARTED.

Are you RUFF-RUFF READY?

POLICE CONE HUNT!

Help police pup Chase sniff out 12 cones hidden on pages throughout the book! **Tick them below as you track them down.**

It's an Emergency!

Ryder's PupPad has just beeped with an urgent message. What does it say? **Use the code to find out – quick!**

CODE KEY

C	E	I	M	N	O	R	S	T	U	V	W	K

Who sent the message to Ryder? **Unscramble the letters.**

K E J A

Pup Search

All paws on deck! Gather the pups by finding their names in the grid. **Look forward, back, up, down and diagonally.**

B	C	H	A	S	E	B	E	W	Y
H	J	X	U	C	V	S	L	K	S
S	L	M	Z	B	A	Y	C	A	K
T	L	A	S	Z	B	O	X	H	Y
R	A	R	C	R	U	B	B	L	E
A	H	S	W	Q	Y	M	E	Z	X
C	S	H	D	H	T	E	A	U	M
K	R	A	R	C	S	A	R	M	F
E	A	L	A	Y	K	C	O	R	O
R	M	L	W	X	J	X	O	Y	G

CHASE

MARSHALL

SKYE

RUBBLE

ROCKY

ZUMA

Can you **find** a jungle pup hiding in the grid, too?

ANSWERS ON **PAGE 75**

Busy Pups

The PAW Patrol are straight into action, and they're giving a yelp for help! **Can you help them solve the puzzles?**

HAT CHASE

FINISH

START

Help Chase through the maze to get his paws on his police hat.

WORD TOWER

Can you help Rubble on the double? **Build this word tower by adding a new letter on each line to create a new word.**

A
A __
__ A T
C A __ T
C R A T __

10

TRASH STASH

How many plastic bottles does Rocky still need to put in the recycle bin?

ODD SKYE OUT

A   **B**   **C**   **D**

This pup's gotta fly! **Which picture of Skye is the odd one out?**

ANSWERS ON **PAGE 75**

Profile: RYDER

The PAW Patrol is on the job!

NAME: Ryder

AGE: 10

ROLE: Leader of the *PAW Patrol*

GADGETS: PupPad

VEHICLE: ATV, which has a Hovercraft mode and Snowmobile mode

SKILLS: Pup training, problem-solving, gadget fixing

CATCHPHRASE:
'No job is too BIG, no pup is too SMALL!'

DID YOU KNOW?

Ryder's jacket is a high-tech gadget, too! **It can transform into a life jacket during water missions.**

Let's Draw Ryder!

Ryder's on a roll. **Copy the picture of the PAW Patrol leader, using the grid to guide you.**

Now colour Ryder so he's ready for the next adventure!

PART 1
MIGHTY MISSIONS

A meteor has landed in Adventure Bay and given the pups mysterious powers! **Help the Mighty Pups on their missions to save the day.**

SUPER SLEDGE

Which path will lead Mighty Everest down the mountain to a soft, snowy landing?

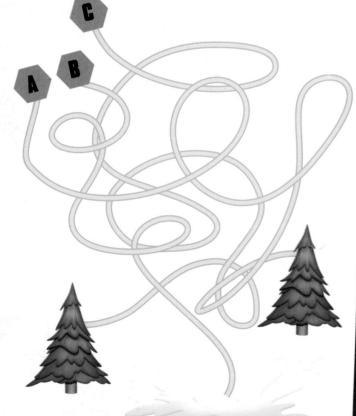

IN A SPIN

Cross out every second letter and then write the remaining letters below to reveal Chase's Mighty power.

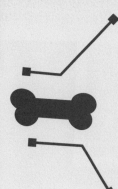

PUP PAIRS

Draw lines to match the Mighty Pup pairs.
Which pup doesn't have a match?

ANSWERS ON **PAGE 75**

15

Profile: CHASE

His NOSE knows!

NAME: Chase

BREED: German Shepherd

ROLE: Police pup

UNIFORM COLOUR: Blue

GADGETS: Pup Pack with megaphone, searchlight and a net that can shoot out to catch things

VEHICLE: Police truck

SKILLS: Directing traffic, blocking dangers, solving mysteries

CATCHPHRASE:

CHASE IS ON THE CASE!

DID YOU KNOW?

Chase can sniff out anything – **but he's allergic to cats and feathers!**

Where's Chase?

Chase is hiding. **Can you find him in the grid?**

Tick off these items as you spot them.

  Chase's bowl

  Bone pup treat

  Chase's badge

ANSWERS ON **PAGE 75**

Pups-in-Training

Ryder is helping the pups practise for their next mission.
Can you find the objects in the scene?
Colour a bone for each object you spot.

What's the name of the PAW Patrol headquarters?
Tick your answer:

The Pup Palace [ ]   **The Lookout** [ ]   **The Watchtower** [ ]

Ruff-Ruff Rides

Pups away! Unscramble the pups' names and then draw lines to match each pup to their PAWsome vehicle.

1 KYORC
A

2 KYES
B

3 SHEAC
C

4 BLUBRE
D

5 SMARLALH
E

ANSWERS ON **PAGE 75**

Design a Pup Ride

Draw a new vehicle for your favourite pup!

Vehicle name: ....

Best for: Land ☐   Air ☐   Water ☐   Other ☐

Special gadgets: ....

....

Profile: MARSHALL

He's all fired up!

NAME: Marshall

BREED: Dalmatian

ROLE: Fire pup and Medic pup

UNIFORM COLOUR: Red

GADGETS:
Pup Pack with a double-spray fire hose

VEHICLE: Fire engine

SKILLS: Putting out fires, rescuing animals, medical help

CATCHPHRASE:

READY FOR A RUFF-RUFF RESCUE!

DID YOU KNOW?

Marshall's medical supplies include an X-ray screen to check pups and people for injuries!

Spot the Pairs

Match the Marshalls! **Draw lines to connect the spotted Dalmatian pairs.**

Trace Marshall's pup tag and give it some FIERY COLOUR.

ANSWERS ON **PAGE 75**

DIVE RIGHT IN

Ready, set, get Mighty wet!
**Which picture is an exact
match for Zuma?**

1

2

3

4

5

Who is Zuma's
flying pup friend?

Y S K E

_ _ _ _

MIGHTY MAZE

Help Rubble blast his way through the maze to meet Rocky for their mighty mission!

START

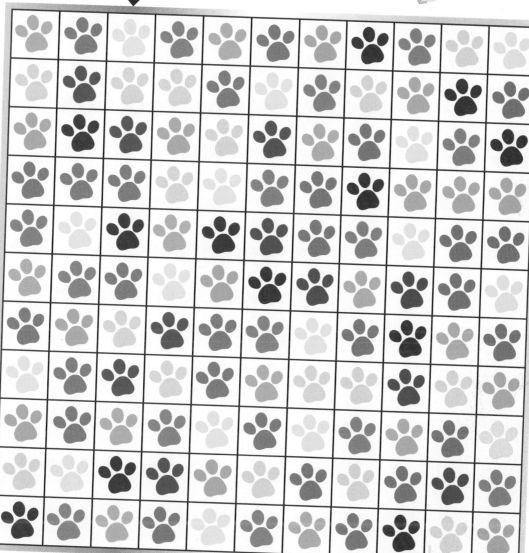

FINISH

Follow the paw prints in this order to find your way.

ANSWERS ON **PAGE 75**

25

Profile: SKYE

Pups away!

NAME: Skye

BREED: Cockapoo

ROLE: Pilot pup

UNIFORM COLOUR: Pink

GADGETS: Pup Pack with wings that allow her to take flight

VEHICLE: Helicopter

SKILLS: Flying, flips and spins!

CATCHPHRASE:

THIS PUP'S GOTTA FLY!

DID YOU KNOW?

Skye is really brave and very little frightens her, **but one thing she is afraid of is eagles.**

Dot-to-dot-apoo!

Join the dots to reveal your favourite Cockapoo as she soars through the sky.

DOODLE some clouds and birds
in the sky around the pup.

Pups at Play

Pups that play together, stay together! **Can you match the missing jigsaw pieces to the scene?**

How many rabbits can you spot in the picture?

1
2
3
4
5

Profile: RUBBLE

Let's dig it!

NAME: Rubble

BREED: Bulldog

ROLE: Construction pup

UNIFORM COLOUR: Yellow

GADGETS: Pup Pack with a bucket arm scoop

VEHICLE: Digger with a bucket shovel and drill

SKILLS: Building, digging, lifting and transporting heavy things

CATCHPHRASE:

HERE COMES RUBBLE, ON THE DOUBLE!

DID YOU KNOW?

Rubble loves to get covered in mud and then visit Katie's Pet Parlour for a warm bubble bath!

I Can Dig It!

A road is blocked with big boulders. **No trouble, just call Rubble!**

How many boulders does he still need to move?

Can you spot this rock in the pile?

There are ☐ **boulders.**

ANSWERS ON **PAGE 76**

Pup Treat Patterns

What treat comes next in each line?

A   B   C   D

1

2

3

4

5

Shadow Shapes

Draw lines to match the pups to their shadows!

Which pup do you think this shadow belongs to?

ANSWERS ON **PAGE 76**

Profile: ROCKY

Rocky to the rescue!

NAME: Rocky

BREED: Mixed breed

ROLE: Recycling pup

UNIFORM COLOUR: Green

GADGETS: Pup Pack with a mechanical claw and lots of handy tools

VEHICLE: Recycling truck

SKILLS: Creativity and ideas, fixing things, solving problems

CATCHPHRASE:

DON'T LOSE IT – REUSE IT!

DID YOU KNOW?

Rocky doesn't like getting wet at all, **which means bath time isn't much fun!**

Don't Lose It!

Rocky is sorting his recycling into groups. Pick out the green bottles and write the letters on the lines below to read his mystery message.

___ ___ ___ ___ ___

___ ___ ___ ___ ___ ___

Unscramble the letters on the red bottles to reveal a special friend!

___ ___ ___ ___ ___

ANSWERS ON **PAGE 76**

To the Rescue

Pick the items you would choose for these pup-tastic challenges.

1 Ryder needs to get a message to the pups quickly. **What would work best?**

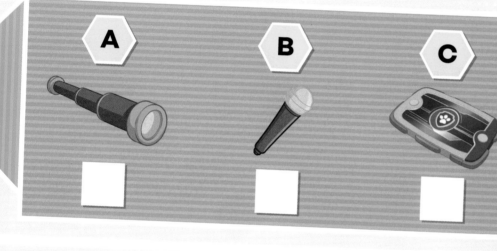

A B C

2 Rocky needs to fix some dangerously loose nails in a go-kart. **What does he need from his pack?**

A B C

3 Help! The pups have an emergency in deep snow.
Which vehicle can get there?

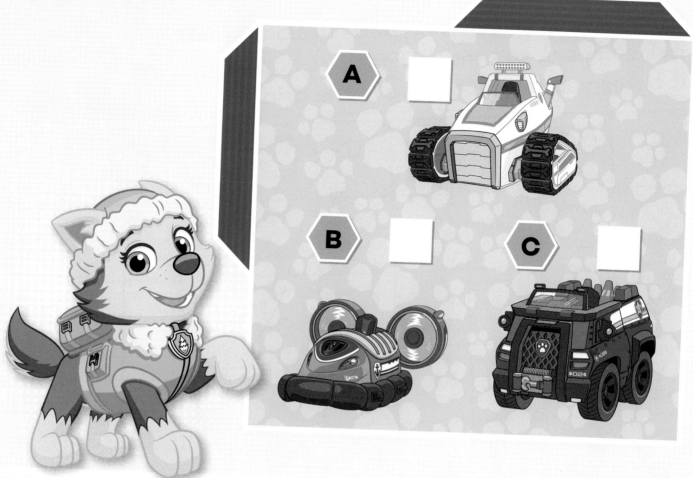

A

B   C

4 Cali is stuck in a tall tree and only Marshall can help.
What item should he bring?

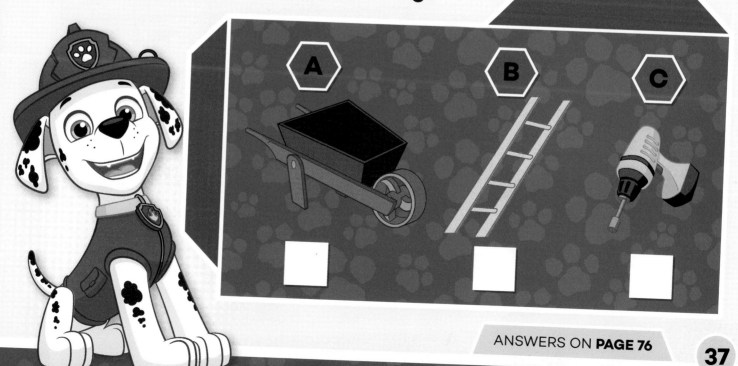

A   B   C

ANSWERS ON **PAGE 76**

Tag Time Trial

Chase needs his pup tag for a mission – fast! Ask someone to time you and see how long it takes you to find his tag in the grid.

0-20 SECONDS –super spy!

21-40 SECONDS –PAWfect tracking

41-59 SECONDS – your nose knows

OVER ONE MINUTE – keep practising!

How many times does Rocky's tag appear in the grid?

ANSWERS ON **PAGE 76**

My Pup Tag

Design your own collar tag! It should match your personality and the things you love to do.

Get some pup-spiration!

Name: ....

Hobbies: ....

Three favourite things: 1.................................... 2.................................... 3....................................

39

Profile: ZUMA

Let's dive in!

NAME: Zuma

BREED: Labrador

ROLE: Water-rescue pup

UNIFORM COLOUR: Orange

GADGETS: Pup Pack with air tanks and propellers for diving and swimming underwater

VEHICLE: Hovercraft that can travel on land or water

SKILLS: Rescuing sea animals, underwater missions, water sports

CATCHPHRASE:

READY, SET, GET WET!

DID YOU KNOW?

Zuma's hovercraft can transform into a **submarine** for deep underwater adventures!

Colour Splash

Dive in and draw the other half of Zuma's face.
Awesome work, dude!

Now COPY THE COLOURS so he's a perfect match!

Octopus Lost-opus!

Race with Zuma through these underwater mazes! **Who will be first to reach the lost baby octopus?'**

START

WHAT TO DO:

- Pick a friend for this **mission challenge**.
- Choose a **maze each** and get your pens ready, then count down from five to begin!
- Whoever gets to the middle of the maze first has **rescued the octopus!**

Pass as many friendly seals as possible, **but don't bump into any snappy crocs!**

START

ANSWERS ON **PAGE 76**

PART 2
MIGHTY MISSIONS

Are you ready for some more super-charged puzzles? **Prepare to save the day!**

COUNT ON SKYE

Mighty Skye has put the wind in a spin and is zooming through the air! **How many times does she appear?**

JUST THE OPPOSITE

The Mighty Pups' powers make them faster, stronger and tougher than ever. **What words are the opposite of the words below?**

FAST............................ WET............................

STRONG............................ HEAVY............................

TOP............................ SHALLOW............................

SUPER SUDOKU

Write the correct pups' names in the blank squares to complete the grids. **Each Mighty Pup shown on the grid should appear three times, and only once in each column and row.**

Profile: EVEREST

Born to slide!

NAME: Everest

BREED: Husky

ROLE: Mountain-rescue pup

UNIFORM COLOUR: Turquoise and yellow

GADGETS: Pup Pack with a grappling hook and foldable, rocket-powered snowboard

VEHICLE: Snow plough with a claw to grab large objects, and transport a sledge

SKILLS: Snowy rescues, climbing icy slopes, super-fast snowboarding

CATCHPHRASE:

ICE OR SNOW, I'M READY TO GO!

DID YOU KNOW?

Everest likes **belly-bogganing**, where she slides down the slopes on her belly!

Word Slide

Solve the clues to this slippery word game and get Everest to the bottom of the slope.

1. It forms when water freezes.

2. It falls from the sky when it's very cold.

3. Everest is this breed of dog.

4. Sit on it to slide down a snowy hill.

5. The place where Everest lives with Jake.

6. Everest has a rocket-powered one for extra-fast sliding!

				I		
				N		W
			U			Y
			E	D		
			T			N
	M					
S			B	O		

PupPad Jumble

Ryder's PupPad has gone haywire and the pups' information has been mixed up. **Circle the wrong statements.**

Rubble is a Bulldog.

Skye is a Labrador.

For an air emergency, call on Zuma.

Rubble is the best detective of all the pups.

The best pup for snowy missions is Everest.

Rocky thinks it's best to put everything in the bin.

Are you finished? **HIGH PAW!**

Cali's Crossword

Try this purr-fect puzzle before this hungry cat runs off for another snack!

ACROSS

2. The name of Cali's owner (5)

4. A stick or ball game that the pups play with Ryder (5)

6. The Cap'n who owns a boat called The Flounder (6)

8. A pup who loves to fix things (5)

9. The PAW _ _ _ _ _ _ has saved Cali many times (6)

DOWN

1. The colour of Marshall's uniform (3)

3. _ _ _ _ _ _ _ _ _ Bay, where Cali and the pups live (9)

5. The robot dog invented by Ryder (7)

7. This pup's gotta fly! (4)

ANSWERS ON **PAGE 77**

Profile: **TRACKER**

Buenos dias, PAW Patrol!

NAME: Tracker

BREED: Chihuahua

ROLE: Jungle-rescue pup

UNIFORM COLOUR: Green

GADGETS: Pup Pack with a compass, torch and grappling cables

VEHICLE: Jeep with a special radar tracking system

SKILLS: Jungle rescues, super-hearing (thanks to his big ears!)

CATCHPHRASE:

I'M ALL EARS!

DID YOU KNOW?

Tracker can speak two languages – **English and Spanish.**

Track the PAWprints

Tracker is following a set of paw prints through the rainforest. **Help him along the trail to find his way to the mystery pup!**

START →

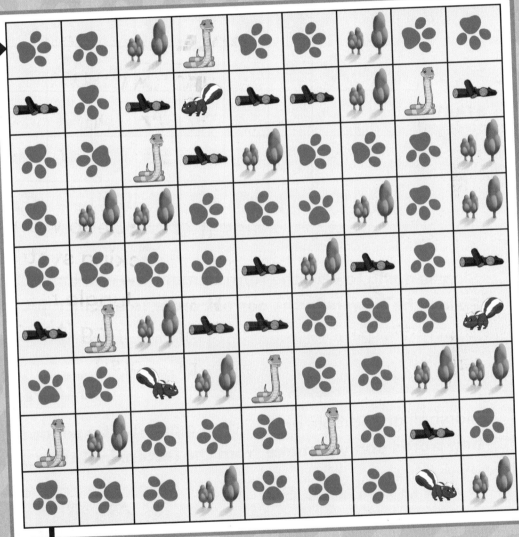

FINISH

Which pup is Tracker tailing?

HINT: This spy pup would usually be the one doing the tracking!

ANSWERS ON **PAGE 77**

Season Adventures

Follow the pups through spring, summer, autumn and winter for fun and games galore.

SPRING

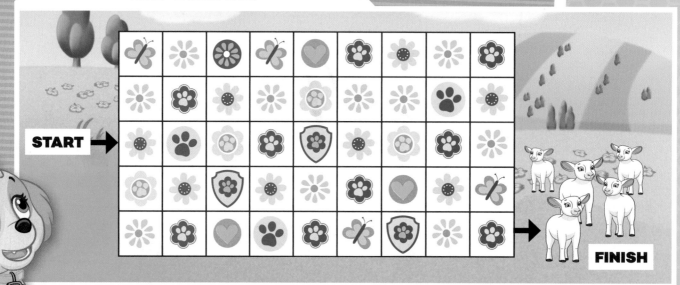

START →

← **FINISH**

Skye is going to visit the farm to meet the new lambs.
Follow the flowers in the correct order to help her get there.

SUMMER

Marshall and Rubble are building a pup-tastic sandcastle. **How many new words can you make from the letters in SANDCASTLE?**

SANDCASTLE

cat

last

AUTUMN

It's harvest time and the pups are helping Farmer Yumi gather the pumpkins. **How many are there?**

WINTER

Chase and Skye are building a snowman on the slopes.
Can you spot five differences between the two pictures?

Profiles:

Ryder and the PAW Patrol do everything they can to keep their friends safe. **Meet some more of the Adventure Bay gang!**

PATROL FRIENDS

KATIE

Katie is Ryder's best friend and runs the Pet Parlour. **She loves to make sure animals are healthy, happy and well-bathed – including her own pet cat named Cali.**

ALEX

Alex is a young boy who doesn't always pay attention, so the PAW Patrol have rescued him more than once! **He runs the Mini-Patrol and would love to be like Ryder one day.**

MR PORTER

Mr Porter is a restaurant owner in Adventure Bay, and also Alex's grandfather. **He's kind, wise and caring towards others.**

JAKE

Jake is a mountain ranger who lives in a snowy chalet and loves to snowboard. **He looks after Everest and knows a lot about animals such as penguins and deer.**

MAYOR GOODWAY

Mayor Goodway is the mayor of Adventure Bay, proudly following in the footsteps of her great-great-great-great-grandfather, Grover Goodway, the first mayor of the town. **She has a pet chicken called Chickaletta.**

FARMER YUMI

Farmer Yumi lives on Fuji Farm and looks after the crops and animals. **The pups often help her out on the farm and she is also their Pup-Fu sensei**

WALLY

Wally is a walrus who lives in The Bay. **He is a talented walrus who loves food, so he enjoys doing tricks for Cap'n Turbot in return for treats!**

My Favourite Pup

Which member of the PAW Patrol is your top hero?
Fill in these pages about your favourite pup.

SECTION 1

My favourite pup is

....
....
....

I like this pup because

....
....
....

SECTION 2

TICK the things you like about your hero!

☆ **BRAVE**

☆ **FAST**

☆ **CLEVER**

☆ **FUNNY**

☆ **LOYAL**

☆ **KIND**

☆ **FRIENDLY**

☆ **PAWSOME!**

Draw a picture of your pup-tastic hero!

PAWtograph of your pup's name:

Who Am I?

SKYE

1

I am a Dalmatian pup.

_____

?

Can you guess who the mystery characters are?

2

I can rescue people and lift them to safety with my vehicle.

_____

?

3

My favourite thing in my Pup Pack is a rocket-powered snowboard.

_____

?

CALI

MARSHALL

4 I live with my owner, Katie, in her Pet Parlour.

?

MAYOR GOODWAY

5 I am the leader of the PAW Patrol.

?

EVEREST

6 I have an important job in Adventure Bay and my pet is called Chickaletta.

?

ANSWERS ON **PAGE 77**

RYDER

SPOT THE DIFFERENCE

Can you spot six differences between these pictures of the Mighty Pups?

1

2

Colour a meteor blast for each one you find.

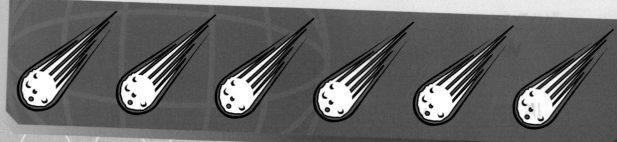

ODD PUPS OUT

Which Mighty pup picture is a little different to all the others?

1

2

3

4

What is Mighty Skye's special power?

POWER JUMP **WIND CONTROL** **SUPER HEARING**

ANSWERS ON **PAGE 77**

On the Farm

The pups are helping Farmer Yumi as she prepares for the weekly market. **Can you answer the questions about the scene?**

1 *How many LAMBS are in the picture?*

2 *Which DIGGER PUP is missing?*

3 *How many CARROTS can you count?*

4 *There is a pile of ANOTHER TYPE OF VEGETABLE – what is it?*

5 *What kind of BUG can you spot in the picture?*

Can you spot these pictures in the scene? **Tick them when you find them.**

ANSWERS ON **PAGE 77**

Sweet Dreams

The pups are ready for bed after a busy day of rescues.
Draw lines to connect the sleepy pup pairs.

Colour the pictures and send the pups to sleep.

ANSWERS ON **PAGE 77**

On a Colour Roll!

Colour this picture of Ryder and Rubble – using a dice! You will also need yellow, blue, green, red and brown pens. Choose the area you will colour then roll a dice to find out what pen colour to use. **See what wild picture you end up with!**

COLOURS

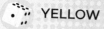 YELLOW   RED

 BLUE   BROWN

 GREEN   LEAVE WHITE

Mighty Door Hanger

Create a door hanger that's pawsome, just like the pups.

WHAT TO DO:

Ask an adult to help you cut out this page along the dotted line.

Ask an adult to cut out the hanger shapes from each side of the page.

Glue one hanger to a piece of card (you can use the back of a cereal packet) and then trim the card.

Glue the other hanger to the back of the card.

Write a message on the front and back of your hanger and it's ready to hang!

Go to page 84 to find the back of your hanger.

JUST YELP FOR HELP

© 2019 Spin Master

Make the PAWsome door hanger and leave messages for visitors to your Lookout!

ONE TEAM

© 2019 Spin Master

Let's Get Tracking

Can you sniff out these jungle pictures? **Tick the items as you spot them.**

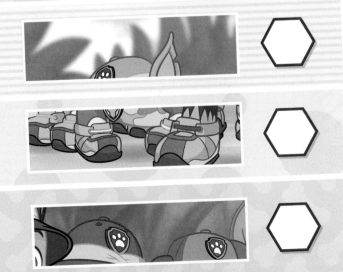

ANSWERS ON **PAGE 77**

Spot the Kit-astrophe!

The Kitty Catastrophe Crew from Foggy Bottom have come to cause trouble for the pups!
Spot eight differences.

Colour a paw for every difference you spot.

Ruff-Ruff Race

The pups are holding a special Pup Games, and only one can win the first place ribbon. **Which pup is the winner of the race?**

Which pup comes 4th?

ANSWERS ON **PAGE 77**

Pup-tastic Quiz!

Are you a *PAW Patrol* superfan? **Pick a pup for each answer in this PAWsome quiz.**

1   **Which pup** wears a **yellow uniform?**

2   **Which pup** has the strongest sense of smell?

3   **Which pup** lives on **Jake's Mountain?**

4 Which pup can be a little clumsy?

....

5 Which pup likes to fly high in her **helicopter?**

....

6 Which pup has an anchor on his pup tag?

....

7 Which pup loves to say, 'Green Means Go!'?

....

Now check your answers and turn over to find your **superfan score!**

ANSWERS ON **PAGE 77**

0-3 correct

Practice makes PAWfect

Get fired up and learn a little more about the pups by trying all the quizzes in this book!

4-6 correct

Itching to know more

Good job. Now, dive back into this book and soon you will have an even more PAWsome score!

7 correct

Totally PAWsome!

Nobody could know more about the **PAW Patrol** than you. You're on a roll!

HIGH PAW!

Answers

Did you find all the hidden cones? They can be found on pages **12, 17, 19, 20, 24, 31, 34, 40, 49, 58, 65,** and **70.**

PAGE 8

Everest stuck in snow storm, JAKE.

PAGE 9

Tracker is also in the grid.

PAGES 10-11

1.

2. A, AT, CAT, CART, CRATE,
3. 10, **4.** C.

PAGES 14-15

1. Path B, **2.** Super speed,
3. Rocky doesn't have a match.

PAGE 17

PAGES 18-19

The Lookout.

PAGE 20

1. Rocky - C, **2.** Skye - D,
3. Chase - E, **4.** Rubble - B,
5. Marshall - A.

PAGE 23

PAGE 24

4,
Skye.

PAGE 25

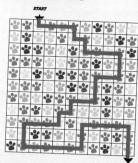

75

PAGES 28-29

There are 6 rabbits.

PAGE 31

21 boulders.

PAGE 32

1. B, **2.** D, **3.** C, **4.** A, **5.** C.

PAGE 33

The shadow belongs to Skye.

PAGE 35

GREEN MEANS GO, Ryder.

PAGES 36-37

1. C,
2. B,
3. A,
4. B.

PAGE 38

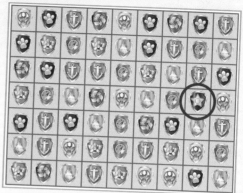

Rocky's tag appears 6 times.

PAGES 42-43

PAGES 44-45

1. 14 times, **2.** Fast/Slow, Strong/Weak, Top/Bottom, Wet/Dry, Heavy/Light, Shallow/Deep,
3.

PAGE 47

1. Ice,
2. Snow,
3. Husky,
4. Sledge,
5. Mountain,
6. Snowboard.

PAGE 48

Rubble is a Bulldog.

Skye is a Labrador.

For an air emergency, call on Zuma.

Rubble is the best detective of all the pups.

Rocky thinks it's best to put everything in the bin.

The best pup for snowy missions is Everest.

PAGE 49
ACROSS: 2. Katie, **4.** Fetch, **6.** Turbot, **8.** Rocky, **9.** Patrol.

DOWN: 1. Red, **3.** Adventure, **5.** Robodog, **7.** Skye.

PAGE 51
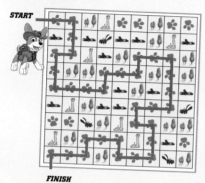

Tracker is trailing Chase.

PAGES 52-53
Spring

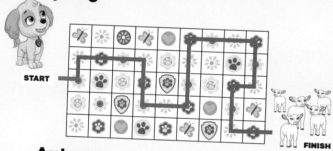

Autumn
17 pumpkins.
Winter

PAGES 58-59
1. Marshall, **2.** Skye, **3.** Everest, **4.** Cali, **5.** Ryder, **6.** Mayor Goodway.

PAGE 60

PAGE 61
3.

Wind control.

PAGES 62-63
1. 3 lambs, **2.** Rubble, **3.** 10 carrots, **4.** Pumpkins, **5.** Ladybird.

PAGES 64-65

PAGE 69

PAGE 70

PAGE 71
Marshall is the winner, Rubble comes 4th.

PAGES 72-74
1. Rubble, **2.** Chase, **3.** Everest, **4.** Marshall, **5.** Skye, **6.** Zuma, **7.** Rocky.